THE WISH

POEMS OF CONTEMPORARY KOREA

THE
WISH

POEMS OF CONTEMPORARY KOREA

Translations by Lee Sun-ai
Edited by Lee Sun-ai and Don Luce

This book is dedicated to
those who wrote and gathered the poems,
and stood for what the poems represent.
We salute them.

ƒ FRIENDSHIP PRESS • NEW YORK

Library of Congress Cataloging in Publication Data

The Wish

  1. Korean poetry — 20th century — Translations
into English. 2. English poetry — Translations from
Korean.
I. Park, Sun Ai. II. Lee, Sun Ai, 1930-
III. Luce, Don.
PL984.E3W57 1983   895.7'14   83-18480
ISBN 0-377-00136-8

ISBN 0-377-00136-8
Editorial Office: 475 Riverside Drive, Room 772, New York, N.Y. 10115
Distribution Office: P.O. Box 37844, Cincinnati, OH 45237
Copyright © 1983 Friendship Press, Inc.
Printed in the United States of America

TABLE OF CONTENTS

Introduction

THE LAND

THE WOMEN

THE CHILDREN

THE STUDENTS

THE WORKERS

INTRODUCTION

Koreans love poetry. Poetry is not just for intellectuals. Workers, students and farmers read and recite their country's poems long into the night. Reading their poetry is one of the best ways to understand Korean history, culture and, of course, inner feelings.

These are the poems of the young and the old. They are the poems of young brides and workers old beyond their years. They express the hopes and sorrows of the people in a land torn apart. There's not a lot of joy in the poems—sorrow comes too easily in a divided country where secret police seem to be on every corner. But there is love—so tender and so deep you can feel it half a world away. Tragically, so often the love is for a family member who has taken the "dusty road to Seoul to sell (her) body," or someone dying from the economic exploitation of the factories.

We feel close to the writers as they tell their stories—we find our hand unconsciously reaching out as we read Kim Min-ki's "Wish Someone Told Me So":

Ah, wish someone held my hand
Ah, wish I held your hand
A high wall blocks the way between us
Ah, wish someone held me so

Many of the poets must remain anonymous. Their truth is too brutal for those in power. Some, like Kim Chi-ha, have used their own names and suffered long years in prison. Some of the poems are simply signed "a textile worker" or "a factory worker."

Adaptation, a more accurate word than translation, of poetry into another language is difficult. Subtle relations between sound and sense, plays on words, and historical allusions are hard to transfer from one language and culture to another. But, we hope we have been able to preserve something of the Korean spirit. Certainly the poems communicate a far different story from the press releases of U.S. military and political visitors that are so often copied verbatim in newswire stories datelined Seoul.

How different Washington's policies might be if the decision-makers would take the time to read these poems. They would, perhaps, understand the depth of nationalism that has opposed foreign intervention for so many years.

They would also understand the longing for unification:

    Water is one, the sun is one, the land is one
    Mountain chains run in one
    Everyone is the descendant of Tan-Goon

No attempt has been made to make this a complete collection. First of all, none of the poems are from north Korea. Many of the great poets, too numerous to mention, are not included. We have, however, included poems from one of Korea's great poets, Kim Chi-ha. We regret that we could not include all the struggle poems of those who have sacrificed so much including prison, torture and even death.

Many of the materials contained in this anthology are from three books published in south Korea: *The Young Jesus*, edited by the youth department of the Christ Presbyterian Church; *The Working Children*, edited by a school teacher, Lee O-Duck; and *The Labor and Songs*, edited and published by the Korean Christian Research Institute for People's Education. Several poems are collected, however, from other sources, particularly from individuals who have sent them out of Korea by visitors to their country.

Many people must be thanked. First and foremost we wish to thank the poets who wrote the poems. We thank, and admire the courage of, those many friends who gathered the poems inside Korea and sent them to us. For reasons of their safety, we cannot mention them by name. There are many in the United States who have given help and encouragement that deserve special mention: Bill Nottingham, Ed Luidens, Pat Patterson, Kim In-shik and Koo Choon-whe.

It is our hope that this volume of poetry will give a voice internationally to Koreans from all walks of life: farmers, students, workers, homemakers, children. It is our belief that a careful listening to their voices will save all of us from repeating many mistakes of the past.

Lee Sun-ai
Don Luce

THE LAND

Wishing fervently for Peace
Stepping on this firey hot earth
The soles of my feet are burning

The southern half of Korea has been the traditional rice basket of the country. Farmers from Chol-La, Kyung-Sang and Choong-Chung provinces have given the nation much of its food. But due to the system of land ownership and other forms of exploitation, the farmers with small land holdings historically have been exploited. This became even worse during the time of the Japanese when large quantities of the harvest were taken to Japan and the farmers were actually left to starve.

After liberation from the Japanese, little was done in the south to change the roots of rural poverty. And a new policy was introduced. In order to keep wages low in the cities to produce cheap exports, the regimes relied more and more on U.S. surplus grain and other foods to feed the workers. More and more farm people have been forced to move to the cities.

Peace

The earth is Peace
The heart of the earth is Peace
Greater than the sky
Bluer than the ocean
Hotter than the sun
The heart of the earth is Peace
Kissing the earth
The soles of my feet feel unworthy
Absorbing everything
The earth brings grass and flowers
The soles of my feet feel unworthy

It is neither bow, nor sword, nor spear
Nor machine guns, cannons, tanks
The problem is nuclear weapons and electronic weapons
The soles of my feet are angry
At the hands which make those weapons
At the fingers which pry and twist the buttons
The hungry children are crying
In the shadow of this great humanity
The soles of my feet pain and hurt

It is neither bow nor sword nor spear
Nor machine gun, cannon, tank
Nor nuclear weapons, electronic weapons
The problem is Peace
One is Peace
Two is Peace
Three is Peace
It is the heart of God
Saddened by Peace being pushed out
Of the Milky Way and the Star Clouds
It is the heart of God
Wishing fervently for Peace
Stepping on this fiery hot earth
The soles of my feet are burning
Stepping on this blazing earth
The soles of my feet are burning
and my body
The burning sacrifice

by Rev. Moon Ik-hwan

평   화

땅은 평화입니다
땅의 마음은 평화입니다
하늘보다 큰 마음
바다보다 푸른 마음
태양보다 뜨거운 마음
땅의 마음은 평화입니다
땅과 입을 맞추면서
발바닥은 부끄럽습니다
냄새나고 더러운 것
무엇하나 마다 않고 받아 마시며
피워내는 풀꽃들
발바닥은 부럽습니다

활이 아닙니다
칼도 창도 아닙니다
기관총도 대포도 탱크도 아닙니다
핵무기 전자무기가 문제입니다
그 가공할 살인무기를 만드는 손들
그 단추를 누르는 것이 자랑스러운 손가락들
발바닥은 분노합니다
위대한 인류의 위대한 문명의 그늘 아래서
배고파 우는 아이들의 울음소리
발바닥은 아프고 쓰립니다
활이 아닙니다
칼도, 창도 아닙니다
기관총도, 대포도, 탱크도 아닙니다
핵무기도 전자무기도 아닙니다
평화가 문제입니다

하나도 평화 둘도 평화, 셋도 평화입니다
은하 성운 밖으로 밀려나는 평화를 보며
슬퍼하는 하느님의 마음입니다
평화를 애타게 바라는
하느님의 뜨거운 마음입니다
간절한 땅을 딛고 서서
발바닥은 불이 됩니다
뜨거운 땅을 딛고 서서
발바닥은 불이 됩니다
몸은 선채로 타는 제물이 됩니다

1982년 늦봄 문 익 환

4

With Whom Do Farmers Talk?

With whom do farmers talk?
With whom do farmers talk?
When they feel resentful and oppressed
with whom do they talk?

A red moon is rising
from a machine over the mountain.
The red moon seems to pour itself all over.
The red moon from above
covers all of the village.
And the farmer's back becomes more stooped.

With whom do farmers talk?
With whom do farmers talk?
When life is dark and painful
with whom do they talk?

Farmers talk with their own wounds.
They talk with the blood and pus in the wounds.
When there is no one to share dialogue,
are they talking to their own body
pressed and weary from too much work and illness?

by Kim Joon-tai

농사꾼은 누구와 말하고 사는가

농사꾼은 누구와 말하고 사는가
농사꾼은 누구와 말하고 사는가
사는 일이 억울하고 답답할 때
농사꾼은 누구와 말하고 사는가

붉은 달이 떠오른다
산너머 機械속에서
쏟아질 듯 떠 오르는 붉은 달
붉은 달은 마음을 내리덮어
더욱 허리가 구부러진 농사꾼

농사꾼은 누구와 말하고 사는가
농사꾼은 누구와 말하고 사는가
사는 일이 캄캄하고 쓰라릴 때
농사꾼은 누구와 말하고 사는가

농사꾼은 자기의 상처와 말한다
상처에 고여있는 피고름과 말한다
아무도 대화를 나누어주지 않을때
일에 골병들어 쭈그러질대로 쭈그러진
자기의 몸뚱이와 말하며 사는가

- 김 준 태-

Drought

Passing by reed bushes
I enter a mountain road
Crossing over several hills
a wide space unfolds
The flowers on the road side
How pretty they are!
The cold breeze in the air
seems hard to be subdued
Eheya ilaria ilarinanda eheya
I go with an empty A-frame* on my shoulder
with a reed in my mouth

Due to the long drought
the farm land is cracked
On dried lanes in the rice fields
field mice run wild alone
Bamboo, bamboo, how sad is your death!
On the roofs of old houses
even the moss is dried up
Eheya ilaria ilarinanda eheya
I go with an empty A-frame on my shoulder
with a reed in my mouth

When shall this drought be over
Perhaps followed by flood!
Heya heya! Merciless weather
It doesn't know how to temper its fury
Walk, walk, my walk of apathy
Eheya Hoong hoong
overwhelmed by sorrow

by Kim Min-ki

---

*The A-frame is used to carry loads—in this case, hopefully, materials scavenged from the countryside.

가 뭄

길 숲 지나서 산길로 접어 들어라
몇구비 넘으니 넓은 곳이 열린다
길 섶에 피인 꽃 어찌 이리도 고우냐
공중에 찬 바람은 잠잘 줄을 모르난가
에헤야 얼라리야 얼라리난다 에헤야
텅빈 지게에 갈잎 물고 나는간다

오랜 가뭄에 논도 밭도 다 갈라지고
메마른 논두렁엔 들쥐들만 기어간다
죽죽 대나무야 어찌 이리도 죽었냐
옛집 추녀엔 이끼마저 말라 버렸네
에헤야 얼라리야 얼라리난다 에헤야
텅빈 지게에 갈잎 물고 나는 간다

이 가뭄 언제나 끝나 무슨 장마도 지려나
해야해야 무정한 놈아 잦을 줄을 모르난가
걸걸 걸음아 무심한 이내 걸음아
흥흥 흥겹다 설음에 겨워 흥겹다
에헤야 얼라리야 얼라리난다 에헤야
텅빈 지게에 갈잎 물고 나는 간다

김 민 기

Love Song of the Earth

I am the earth
lying long and empty
Who plowed and turned over my bosom?
Who put land marks in my bosom?

I am lying again today
suffering pain
Many hands fumble and exploit
Many fall quiet
on my shy nude body at dawn
Dirty soles of farmers' feet
kiss my unguarded bosom

My body is loved at their whims
Over the dawn of earthy yellow desire
timid fog falls down as a night gown
And my seeds sprout
in a tender sleep

Sputtering sounds of urination
Noise of building fences everywhere
Digging holes here and there
Land marks of greed are pushed in
every morning in my tender bosom

Another dawn, a feeble cry
Treading on pains
Who is it that coughs?
In my bosom are raised seeds of sorrow
Fed upon the urination of 5,000 years
and the tears of working people
Who is it that put iron wires in my bosom?

Love me, lying long
Open wide my lean bosom
Immersing in the earthy yellow daylight
Sow the seeds of bright hope
In my aged wounded bosom
That awaits tender hands
Of my true love so beautiful!

After straw shoes have trespassed
After rubber shoes have trespassed
After military boots have trespassed
After gnawing tanks have trespassed
I am still the earth, the painful flesh

Under the sputtering sound of urination
Under all sorts of trash and spit
I am still the clean earth
the bearer of pain
no one can heal yet
Today who painted colors on this land?
Today who put demarkation so willfully?
The land that raises a thread of pains
Silently in spite of many trespasses
Under the soles torn and unclean
Fed on dung and blood, fresh and thick
Of the people so good
Under the footsteps of enriched history
The earth is crying pungent tears

by Moon Byung-lan

땅의 戀歌

나는 땅이다
길게 누워 있는 빈 땅이다
누가 내 가슴을 갈아 엎는가?
누가 내 가슴에 말뚝을 박는가?

아픔을 참으며
오늘도 나는 누워 있다
수많은 손들이 더듬고 파헤치고
내 수줍은 새벽의 나체 위에
가만히 쓰러지는 사람
농부의 때묻은 발바닥이
내 부끄런 가슴에 입을 맞춘다

멋대로 사랑해버린 나의 육체
황토빛 욕망의 새벽 우으로
수줍은 안개의 잠옷이 내리고
연한 잠 속에서
나의 씨앗은 새 순이 돋힌다

철철 오줌을 갈기는 소리
곳곳에 새끼줄을 치는 소리
여기저기 구멍을 뚫고
새벽마다 연한 내 가슴에
욕망의 말뚝을 박는다

상냥하게 비명을 지르는 새벽녘
내 아픔을 밟으며
누가 기침을 하는가,
5천년의 기나긴 오줌을 받아 먹고
걸걸한 백성의 눈물을 받아 먹고
슬픈 씨앗을 키워온 가슴
누가 내 가슴에다 철조망을 치는가?

나를 사랑해다오, 길게 누워
황토빛 대낮 속으로 잠기는
앙상한 젖가슴 풀어 헤치고
아름다운 주인의 손길 기다리는
내 상처받은 묵은 가슴 위에
빛나는 희망의 씨앗을 심어다오 !

짚신이 밟고 간 다음에도
고무신이 밟고 간 다음에도
군화가 짓밟고 간 다음에도
탱크가 으렁으렁 이빨을 갈고 간 다음에도
나는 다시 땅이다 아픈 맨살이다

철철 갈기는 오줌 소리 밑에서도
온갖 쓰레기 가래침 밑에서도
나는 다시 깨끗한 땅이다
아무도 손대지 못하는 아픔이다

오늘 누가 이땅에 빛깔을 칠하는가 ?
오늘 누가 이땅에 멋대로 線을 긋는가 ?
아무리 밟아도 소리하지 않는
갈라지고 때묻은 발바닥 밑에서
한줄기 아픔을 키우는 땅
어진 백성의 똥을 받아 먹고
뚝뚝 떨어지는 진한 피를 받아 먹고
더욱 기름진 역사의 발바닥 밑에서
땅은 뜨겁게 뜨겁게 울고 있다

THE WOMEN

Over the white hill, black hill, thirsty hill
On the dusty road to Seoul
I go to sell my body

In traditional Korea with its age-old Confucian practice, the oppression of women permeates almost every walk of life. This is especially true in the marriage system where the young woman is removed from her family to live with the husband's family as their servant and to bear sons to continue the family tree. Modernization and industrialization have further complicated the plight of women. Industrialization has created massive social dislocation. Modern materialism has encouraged the profiteering off women.

Women, and men, have not been quiet; modernization has also brought new ideas and demands for freedom. So the women in these poems do not take their plight quietly!

Gold Chain, Silver Chain

A sigh at midnight
to whom is it addressed?
To have been born a woman
is it sinful to sigh?
No, no more please.
Can it be sinful to be born?
Let's gather all the sighs
and cry out loud.

Dark eyes of the passing girl
are covered with clouds.
Today's clouds, rain clouds
snow clouds, black clouds
No, no more please.
Today's clouds can't be lifted,
just sitting there
Let's take them away
with two arms out-stretched.

In the morning wind, cold wind
a crying grandmother passes by
All the tears she has shed in life
white tears and black tears.
No, no more please.
She wept all her life
She can't cry any more
Wipe the tears and raise her head.

A baby girl plays in the flower garden.
Who is running after you?
Binding chains of thousands of years
gold chains, silver chains
No, no more please.
I can only live breaking
chains of thousands of years
Be courageous, be courageous.

Anonymous

금사슬   은사슬

한밤중에 짓는 한숨 누굴보고 한숨 짓나
여자평생 태어난죄 짓는 것이 한숨인가
아뇨마오 더는마오 태어난 죄 어디있나
짓는것은 한테모아 큰소리로 외쳐보고

저기 가는 저 아가씨 흐린 눈에 구름꼈네
오늘 하루 덮인 구름 눈비구름 먹빛구름
아뇨 마오 더는 마오 오늘 하루 덮인 구름
앉아서는 못 걷겠네 두 팔 벌려 걸어보고

아침 바람 찬 바람에 울고 가는 저 할머니
한 평생을 흘린 눈물 검은 눈물 하얀 눈물
아뇨마오 더는마오 한 평생을 흘린 눈물
이제는 더 못 울겠네 눈물 닦아 고개들고

꽃밭에만 노는 아가 누가 너를 잡더느냐
천만년을 묶인 사슬 금사슬에 은사슬에
아뇨마오 더는마오 천만년을 묶인 사슬
끊고 봐야 나 살겠네 힘들내여 힘들내여

Playboy of Chin-Ju

I lived three years in my in-laws' home
a house with no fence nor wall around.
One day my mother-in-law said to me.
Baby, baby, my daughter-in-law,
your man of Chin-Ju is coming home.
Go to the Chin-Ju South River to wash clothes.

I went to the Chin-Ju South River.
The mountains are beautiful, the river is good.
I wielded the washing stick with all my force,
udang, tang, tang, tang.
Suddenly a horse's gallop was heard
I saw him at a side glance
He wore a heavenly hat,
riding on a horse like a cloud.
He passed me by as if unnoticed.

I washed white clothes white,
I washed black clothes black.
As I came home
the living quarters were noisy.

My mother-in-law said to me
Child, baby, my daughter-in-law
your man of Chin-Ju came back home.
So go into the living quarters.

I went into the living quarters
I found a tableful of wines and liquors
With a concubine under his arm,
he was singing wine songs.

I came down to my room,
and took nine kinds of drugs.
I cut three yards of silk
and hung myself.

My man from Chin-Ju heard the story.
He came out in his socks and mourned.
I never thought you could do this.
Oh, my love, oh, my love.

Love with a Ki-saeng lasts three years
Love with a wife lasts hundreds of years.
I never thought you could do this.
I never thought you could do this.

Anonymous

진주 난봉가

울도 담도 없는 집에서 시집살이 삼년만에

시어머니 하시는 말씀 애야 아가 며늘아가
진주낭군 오실 터이니 진주남강 빨래가라

진주남강 빨래가니 산도 좋고 물도 좋아
우당탕탕 두들기는데 난데없는 말굽소리

곁눈으로 힐끗보니 하늘같은 갓을쓰고
구름같은 말을 타고서 못본듯이 지나더라

흰 빨래는 회개 빨고 검은 빨래 검게 빨아
집이라고 돌아오니 사랑방이 소요허다

시어머니 하시는 말씀 애야 아가 며늘아가
진주낭군 오셨으니 사랑방에 들러가라

사랑방에 올라보니 온갖가지 술을 놓고
기생첩을 옆에 끼고서 권주가를 부르더라

건넌방에 내려와서 아홉가지 약을 먹고
비단 석자 베어내어 목을 매어 죽었더라

진주낭군 이말듣고 버선발로 뛰어나와
너 이럴줄 내몰랐다 사랑 사랑 내사랑아

화류객정은 삼년이요 본댁 정은 백년인데
너 이럴줄 내몰랐다 사랑 사랑 내사랑아

Kwang-Ju Sister

My sister became widowed at nineteen
At mid-night men rushed in with their dirty boots.
At mid-night in the newly-weds room.
They've taken away my sleeping brother-in-law.
He died together with the gang and lies decayed
at the edge of Moo-Dong Mountain under a rock.
But he comes back every night limping.
My sister became a widow at nineteen
She grabbed the bayonet crying and fell.
She spends all her life, falling and crying.
My poor sister, Kwang-Ju sister.

by Yang Sung-woo

Road to Seoul

I go, don't cry
Over the white hill, black hill, thirsty hill
On the dusty road to Seoul
I go to sell my body
Without the promise of when I'll return
A homecoming full of smiles one day
When ribbon grass blooms in full
I go, don't cry, I go
Even though the world is cruelly cruel
Can I ever forget the fragrance of
Barley and Marvel of Peru flowers?
I shall never, never forget
I shall return wet with tears
Of dreaming
I shall return following the starlight at night
I go, don't cry, I go
I go to sell my body
On the dusty road to Seoul

by Kim Chi-ha

광주 누님

열아홉에 과부가 된 나의 누님아
한밤중에 흙발로 떼몰려 와서
한밤중에 신방에 떼몰려 와서
잠든 매형을 붙잡아 가던
험상궂은 사람들과 함께 죽어서
산기슭에 썩어, 무등산 바위 밑에
썩어 있다가
매형은 밤마다 절면서 오고
열 아홉에 과부가 된 나의 누님아
총창끝에 매달려 울다 쓰러진
쓰러진 채 한평생을 울다 쓰러진
불쌍한 누님아 광주 누님아

양 성 우

서울길

간다 우지마라 간다
흰고개 검은고개 목마른 고개넘어
팍팍한 서울길 몸팔러 간다

언제야 돌아오리란 언제야 웃음으로 환히
꽃피워 돌아오리란
댕기풀 안스러운 약속도 없이
간다 우지마라 간다
모질고 모진 세상에 살아도
밀냄새가 잊힐까 분냄새가 잊힐까
사뭇사뭇 못잊을 것을
꿈꾸다 눈물 젖어 돌아올 것을
밤이면 별빛따라 돌아올 것을
간다 우지마라 간다
팍팍한 서울길 몸팔러 간다

김 지 하

Milky Way

The ribbons of my sister's Korean dress
were untied
When she was drafted into the Teishintai*
They flutter in night breezes until this day
On the narrow lanes of the rice field
where she was dragged and
pulled by her hair ribbons
Multitudes of ribbon grass grow in spring
But my sister has never come back
She, who left with her rubber shoes
Dragging all the way
All alone I come back
Limping, after pulling weeds in the rice field
Father was beaten to death
as he presented his harvest crop in exchange
he hoped, for his drafted elder son
My mother, chewing pine leaves, died of infection
Full of pus all over
My sister has gone, embracing
All the sorrow of this land
Perhaps you've bitten
The edge of your blouse, my sister
Shedding bloody tears
You haven't come back after the war
Mist hidden under your skirt
You must have borne many loins
while you writhed
Your groans, ejected between teeth
with your eyes firmly closed
biting your tongue compellingly
"Japanese, Korean same Tenoheika**"
Resound from the consternated
Milky Way in the northern sky

by Chong-O

---

*Teishintai literally means "Body Dedication Corps." During World War II Japan
drafted young Korean women to serve as prostitutes for Japanese soldiers at the
front.
**Tenoheika is the Japanese Emperor. These words were used by the young
conscripted prostitutes for the sake of their survival.

은 하 수

정신대간 누부가 끌러 놓았을 옷고름이
시방도 밤이면 펄럭여 보이누나

꽃댕기 쥐어잡혀 끌려가던 논둑에는
봄이와서 댕기풀이 무더기로 돋아나건만
고무신 질질 끌려가며 오지 않는 누부야

나혼자 절름거리며 논매고 돌아온다
대동아 전쟁에 징병간 형님 찾으려고
공출내려갔던 아배는 매 맞아 죽고
솔잎 씹으며 어매는 부황들어 죽어
갈적에 이땅의 슬픔안고 간 누부야

피눈물로 바들 바들 앞섶 물었을 누부야
동란이 지나도 돌아오지 않는 누부야
반물 치마속에 숨겨간 아지랑이 품어내어
수많은 허리 휘감아 몸부림쳤을 누부야
눈 딱 감고 혀 앙 깨문 이빨사이로 뱉어내어
떠돌고 있는 신음소리
'닛뽄징 조센징 덴도 헤이까 나오지네' *
북방하늘 질겁하는 은하수에서 들려오누나

- 하 종 오 -

* '일본인과 조선인은 천황폐하가 같지요' 라는 뜻으로 일제에 강제
매춘당한 우리나라 여성들이 그 비참한 생활속에서도 목숨을 부지
하기 위해 일본 병사에 대한 써비스 용어로 서툴게 사용했다고 함.

THE CHILDREN

I gaze upon the mountain
I see Seoul in my eyes
And I feel tears well up

Most of these poems are from a book called *Working Children*. They were collected in 1978 by a primary school teacher in the rural areas. These poems especially reflect the problems of the rural poor.

Children's poems, like children's drawings, reveal their world simply and without ideological influence or esoteric symbolism. We can see and feel their world of simple smiles and tears. Yet as life becomes more complex, the effects on the young and innocent can be devastating, as you can see in some of these poems.

Blackbird

The blackbird
Stays in stone walls
During the daytime
And steals food
At night
From other people

Nobody knows what he does

When his stomach is filled
He flies to a far-away mountain
Enjoying the scene of heavenly sky
And then flies up into the sky
To dance with the moon and stars

by Chung Boo-keu
3rd Grade Boy
Andong Daegok School

까 만 새

까만 새가
낮에는
돌다물에 들어가 있다가
밤이 되면
아무도 모르게
남의 집 양식을
후배 먹고
배가 둥둥 하면
저 먼 산에 올라가
하늘을 구경한다
그러다가
하늘로 올라가서
달과 별과 춤을 춘다

안동 대곡분교3년 정 부 코 / 68. 11.

「돌다물」돌담. 「후배 먹고」훔쳐 먹고.

Tears

Lunch time at school
Tears don't come to my eyes
I don't cry when my friends see me
But I cry all alone
Having no food for the family
We bear empty stomachs
My little brothers and sisters
Are at the brink of tears from hunger

When I return home from school
The lunch is usual
Cooked cereal mixed with wild herbs
While I study mathematics
I try to convince myself
The best thing for me is to study
But tears flow like rain
From my eyes
As I write my diary

by Lee Dal-soo
5th Grade Boy
Sangjoo Chungli School

My Sister

Following our brother, my sister
has gone to Seoul to work as a maid
I always feel like crying
As I gaze upon the mountain
I see Seoul in my eyes
And I feel tears well up

by Kim Chin-bok
4th Grade Boy
Sang-Ju Chungli School

눈   물

학교에서 점심 시간만 다가오면
나는 눈물이 난다
그래도 동무들이 보는 데는 울지 않아도
나 혼자 울 때가 있다
우리 집에는 양식이 없어
밥을 먹지 않을 때가 많다
집에 돌아와 보면 동생들이
배고파서 울상을 하고 있다
점심도 나물죽을 끓여 먹기 때문에
그런 것이다
산수 예습을 하면서 나는
공부만 잘하면 제일이라고 생각했지만
지금 일기를 쓰고 있는 나의 눈에는
또 눈물이 비 오듯 하는 것이다

상주 청리5년 이 달 수 / 63.5

누   나

누나는 형님 따라
서울로 식모살이 갔다
내 마음은 언제나
울고 싶은 마음
교실에서 산을 바라보면
내 눈에는 서울이 보인다
그러면 눈물이 나올라 한다

상주 청리 4년 김 진 복 / 64.4.20

Father's Illness

Yesterday my father
Went to carry hay on his back
He trembled
As he bound the hay into bundles
And carried the bundles on his shoulders

He took a break on the hill at Sung-Choon's house
And as he was getting up
He bumped his head on a rock behind him
And fell
Rolling into a ditch
With the bundle still fastened on his back

A stranger came to his rescue
Supporting him
As he sat there gasping
His breath stopping
and starting again
over and over

I went there and wept
Looking at the height of the hill

by Kim Kyu-pil
3rd Grade Boy
Andong Daegok School

아버지의 병환

우리 아버지가
어제 풀 지로 갔다
풀을 묶을 때 벌벌 떨렸다고 한다
풀을 다 묶고 나서
지고 오다가
성춘네 집 언덕 위에 쉬다가
일어서는데
뒤에 있는 독맹이에 받혀서

그 높은 곳에서 떨어질 때
풀하고 구불어 내려와서 도랑 바닥에 떨어졌다
짐도 등따리에 지고 있었다
웬 사람이 뛰어와서
아버지를 일받았다
앉아서 헐떡 헐떡 하며
숨도 오래 있다 쉬고 했다 한다
내가 거기 가서
그 높은 곳을 쳐다보고 울었다

안동 대곡분교 3년 김 규 필 / 69. 6. 10

Grandmother

My father drinks all the time
Grandmother went to look for him
Saying to him in tears
"Why do you drink all the time
And do nothing for your family?"

He still drinks
And Grandmother has come home
Not saying a word
Not answering our questions
Sitting motionless in the room

She is sick now
And dying in silence

by Kim Ryong
6th Grade Girl
Moon Kyung School

Mother

My mother works hard every day
Washing, cooking, working in the fields
I feel sad as I think of my mother
When I left home for school this morning
She was chopping leaves for silkworms
She seems always to be sad
How can I live without her?

There is a girl in my village
Who lost her mother
There's no laughter in her family
They get angry, sad
Or cry quietly when very sad

할 머 니

아버지는 술만 잡수시고,
할머니가 찾으러 가서
야야, 너는 집 일은 조금도 보지 않고
술만 먹고 앉았나,
울음 섞인 소리로 말했다
아버지는
그래도 먹고만 있었다
할머니는 집에 와서
우리가 무엇을 물어도
대답도 하지 않고
방에 앉아만 있다
할머니는 아픈 중에
소리 없이 죽어가는 것이다

문경 김 룡 여 / 72. 5. 4

어 머 니

　우리 어머니는 날마다 된 일을 하신다.　빨래하고
밥짓고 뽕 주고 아주 바쁘시다.　어머니 생각하면　슬
프다.　오늘 아침 학교에 올 때도 어머니는 뽕을 쌀고
있었다.　어머니 마음은 언제나 외로운것 같다.　어머
니 죽으면 우쩨 살까.　어머니 잃은 아이가 우리 동네
에 있다.　그 집에는 언제나 웃음 소리는 들리지 않는
다.　성을 내고 울고 아주 슬플 때는 가만히 운다. 그
집 아이가 내 동무였다.　나는 가한테 어머니 보고 싶
지, 하면 눈물을 흘린다.　그 때 한 번 나도 눈물이났
다.　동네 사람이 불쌍하다 하며 머리를 쓰다듬어 준
다.

상주 청리4년 이 순 회 / 64. 5. 25

「쌀고」썰고.　「가한테」그 아이한테.　「우쩨」어떻게

29

The girl is my friend
She wept when I asked her
If she missed her mother
So I wept with her
The villagers caress her hair
In sympathy

by *Lee Soon-hee*
4th Grade Girl
Sangjoo Chungli School

Paper Kite

Let's fly a paper kite
to the end of the sky
Even if my hands cannot reach
to the top of the clouds

Last night mother didn't come home
a lonely letter was waiting
I took the letter to a neighbor
Uncle* sighed after reading it
I couldn't believe what he said
Mother has followed a "hello uncle**"
There is no one to play with
What shall I do?
Shall I run along the railway?
What's the sound from
across the railroad tracks?
Is it a trumpet calling for
a heavenly journey?

Let's fly a paper kite
to the end of the sky
Even if my hands cannot reach
to the top of the clouds

Anonymous

*In Korea, any grown-up male person is called uncle.
**"Hello Uncle" refers to a United States serviceman.

종 이 연

라이라라이라라 이라라이라
라아이라라이라 라이라이라―

종이 연 날래 자 하늘 끝까지 날리자
내 손이 안닿아도 구름위까지

간밤에 어머니 돌아오지 않고
편지만 뎅그마니 놓여 있는데
그 편지 들고서 옆집 가보니
아저씨 보시고 한숨만 쉬네

아저씨 말씀 못 믿어워도
헬로 아저씨 따라 갔다는데
친구도 없네 무얼하고 놀까
철길 따라서 뛰어나볼까

철길 저편에 무슨 소리인가
하늘나라 올라갈 나팔소리인가
종이 연 날리자 하늘 끝까지
내 손이 안닿아도 구름위까지

THE STUDENTS

Where could they be?
What could they be doing
At this time, my friends

The organized student movement has its roots in the 1910-1945 Japanese colonial period. Since then, it has been the main thrust of the people's movement for freedom and democracy. The most famous is the March 1, 1919, Independence Movement. It was a nation-wide uprising, but modern historians give credit to the students for the initial planning and organization. Tens of thousands were massacred, imprisoned and tortured. Even though the mission of independence was not accomplished, the spirit could not be extinguished.

In 1930, a dispute between a Korean student and a Japanese student in Kwang-Ju ignited another nationwide uprising. This, too, was brutally suppressed. Tragically, this would be the site of a government massacre of students and workers demanding democracy 50 years later.

One of the most successful student uprisings toppled the dictatorial regime of Syngman Rhee on April 19, 1960. One of its ringleaders was Korea's famous resistance poet, Kim Chi-ha. Twenty-three years have passed and the hoped-for freedom and democracy have not come.

The student struggle goes on. The youth of today were babies at the time of the demonstrations that toppled Syngman Rhee in 1960. Yet U.S. support for the oppressive regime of Chun Doo Hwan continues year after year—always in the name of anti-communism, economic growth and stability. Out of this continuing historical legacy of pain and suffering come these expressions of wishes, dreams and anger.

The Empty School Yard

Everyone is gone
and in the empty school yard
only Golden Bells are in full bloom

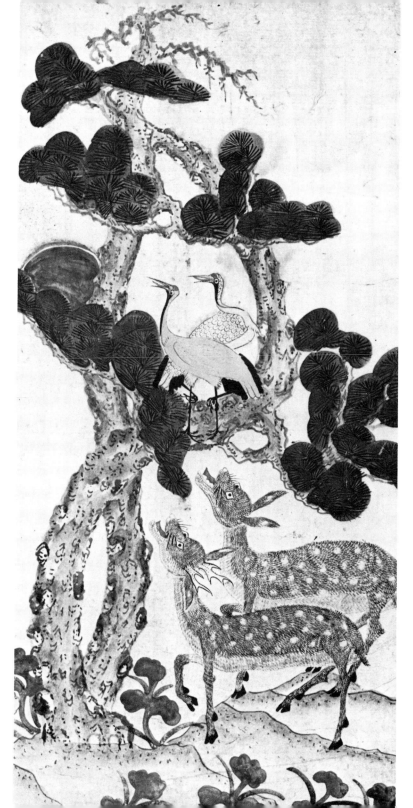

Full of spring rays
falling on empty benches
without laughter of joyous gatherings

Classrooms are covered with dust
The desks and chairs
miss their occupants

Where could they be?
What could they be doing
at this time, my friends!

At home I don't feel comfortable
Out in the field I'm not happy
Hovering thoughts are only of my friends

With the longing of first love
I miss my friends!

Everyone has gone somewhere
and in the empty school yard
only the Golden Bells are in full bloom

by Whang Myung-gul

(Note: This is a typical scene after many protesting students are arrested and the
school is ordered closed.)

Father's Word

"The students threw stones
and the armed police shot tear gas
In the end of pushing and being pushed
hundreds of students were taken
at Kwan-Ak, An-Am-Dong, Shin-Chon and Kwang-Ju*"
Whenever I hear such news
and see you coming home in work clothes
stained with blood
as a father I find no words to say to you
Only my eyelids become hot

빈 교정

모두들 어디가고
빈 교정에
개나리만 만발했나

봄볕 가득한
빈 잔치
빈 벤치

먼 지앉은 교실의
책상 걸상들이
임자를 보고 싶다네

어디 갔을까
무엇하고 있을까
친구들은 지금
집에 있어도 편찮고
산에 가도 언짢아
생각느니 친구들뿐

사랑을 갖 배울때의
그 그리움
그 보고 싶음이어라

모두들 어디가고
빈 교정에
개나리만 만발했나

-황 명 걸-

아버님 말씀

학생들은 돌을 던지고
무장경찰은 최루탄을 쏘아대고
옥신 각신 밀리다가 관악에서도
안암동에서도 신촌에서도
광주에서도
수백명 학생들 연행됐다는
소식을 들을 때마다

Standing at the gate
I feel proud and sad
I have lived all my life
working in the fields
If I tell you to live comfortably
it is to ask you to become a thief
If I tell you to be an honest man
it is to ask you to be poor
like your father
Fearful of the logic of this land
as your father I have to shut my mouth
All my friends who do well in their lives
and even your old mother
who has shared life with me all our years
laugh at my economic inability
They no longer want to listen
to what I have to say
But my son, I have something to tell you
Even as a failure
who wanders around many work sites
Till old age to feed my children
being sensitive to other people's
feelings and need to survive
As a poor man of this land I tell you
My son, never lose bravery
because of poverty
Hate those who are to be hated
Never reckon misfortune as fate
Never forget that you are one flesh
with your poor neighbor
and they are your nation
My son, who still throws stones
and sheds blood!

by Chung Hi-sup

*Kwan-Ak is the site of Koryo University
An-Am-Dong is the site of Seoul University
Shin-Chon is the site of Yonsei and Ewha Women's Universities
Kwang-Ju is the site of a people's uprising and government massacre in May 1980

피묻은 작업복으로 밤늦게
술취해 돌아온 너를 보고
애비는
말 못하고 문간에 서서
눈시울만 뜨겁구나
반갑고 서럽구나
평생을 발붙이고 살아온 터전에서
아들아 너를 보고 편하게 살라하면
도둑놈이 되라는 말이고
너더러 정직하게 살라하면
애비같이 구차하게 살라는 말이 되는
이 땅의 논리가 무서워서
애비는 입을 다물었다마는
이렇다하게 사는 애비친구들도
평생을 살 붙이고 살아온 늙은
에미까지도
이젠 이 애비의 무능한 경제를
대 놓고 비웃을 줄 알고 더 이상
내말에 귀를 기울이지 않는구나
그렇다 아들아 실패한 애비로서
다 늙어 여기저기 공사판을 기웃대며
자식 새끼들 벌어 먹이느라
눈치보는
이땅의 가난한 백성으로서
그래도 나는 할 말을 해야겠다
아들아 행여나 가난에 주눅들지 말고
미운 놈 미워할 줄 알고
부디 네 불행을 운명으로
알지마라
가난하고 떳떳하게 사는 이웃과
네가 언제나 한몸임을 잊지말고
그들이 네 나라임을 잊지 말아라
아직도 돌을 들고
피흘리는 내 아들아

THE WORKERS

Though you face darkness and a steep road
Don't despair! Be courageous and strong!
We will keep the union through our unity.

On March 16, 1961, Park Chung-hee carried out a military coup. Soon after that Park developed an industrialization scheme that began some of the world's worst workers' conditions. The exploitation of the workers intensified after the normalization of relations between Korea and Japan in 1965. To encourage more foreign capital, Park liberalized investment laws. The policies were "liberal" for the foreign owners, but not for the workers. The most important incentive to foreign investment was cheap labor. The emphasis was on producing labor-intensive consumer goods for export. "Our greatest resource is our cheap workers," a government official bragged.

The source of these cheap workers was the rural areas where nearly 75 percent of the population lived in 1965. A series of push-pull factors sent literally millions of young Koreans to the cities. The price of rice was kept artificially low, while fertilizer and equipment costs skyrocketed. And while low incomes pushed the rural youth to leave the farms, the pull of the exciting city life was dramatized by new communications media such as television.

The south Korean government was not the only country offering cheap labor. "You gotta offer cheaper girl than Indonesia if you want the companies to keep coming here," the government official put it crudely.

The young workers saw their labor benefitting the rich:
When the puppy of the company president catches a cold, it is taken to the hospital in a luxurious car.

And they saw themselves in a never-ending struggle to stay alive: "The worker's lot is to take No-Doze, Pep Pills."

Out of their anger of being the worker-machines, comes their cry: "We Will Struggle and Win."

Life of the Workers

Department stores are filled
With the products of my hands
But you cannot see in my tiny space
Even a single out-moded item
What fate made me born a worker
Dispised, mistreated
By a rough world, tough luck
No matter how far I go
No turning point in my life
No matter how hard I work
My reward is sickness
Even a puppy has a home
And doesn't worry about the next meal
Under the sky of this earth
I haven't a room of my own
We are shrunken by the exploitation of the rich
Even sparrows sleep in their nest at night
What crimes have we workers committed in life
That we are forced to endure the noisy machines
Day and night, as soon as we awake
Believing "one day the sun will shine in the rat hole"*
Believing one day I will be better off by sweat and hard work
Sustained in this belief and working hard
But alas! Workers are deceived by the world
A merciless world oppresses the workers
Treating us badly, despising us
They laugh at us, call us names
My heart is resentful in this sad world
I wonder if our arrested union leader is safe
Is she sound and healthy under this same sky
Though you face darkness and a steep road
Don't despair! Be courageous and strong!
We will keep the union through our unity.

Anonymous

---

*A Korean proverb, meaning there is hope even in the worst situation.

노동자의 생활 (쫓간이)

내손 거쳐 만든 물건 백화점에 가득해도
셋방살이 내 방에는 재고품도 하나없네
어쩌다가 이 내 몸은 노동자로 태어나서
거친세상 풍랑속에 멸시천대 받는구나

가도가도 끝이없는 우리네들 인생살이
바둥바둥 애써보아도 남는것은 병뿐이라
강아지도 집이있고 양식걱정 안하는데
하늘아래 이땅위에 방한칸도 내것없네

있는놈들 착취속에 기를못핀 약한우리
참새들도 밤이되면 제집찾아 잠자는데
우리의 노동자는 전생의 무슨죄로
눈만뜨면 기계소리 밤도낮도 구별없네

쥐구멍도 언젠가는 볕뜰날이 있다하고
부지런히 땀흘리면 잘살수도 있다하여
그말듣고 죽자살자 기를쓰며 살은우리
그러나 이세상은 노동자를 속였구나

거친세상 멸시천대 노동자를 짓누르고
농사꾼의 아들딸인 우리들을 억압하면
공돌이라 공순이라 천대하며 비웃는구나
한 맺힌 내가슴아 서러운 이세상아

지부장님 별고없이 하늘아래 몸성한지
온세상이 캄캄하여 나아갈길 험하여도
낙심말고 용기내여 건강하게 지내소서
우리의 노동조합 단결하여 지키리라

Magnolia

White magnolia
Over the fence of Sooni's home
Even under the gorgeous sun-rays of midday
You look sad
Sooni left for Seoul
Pledging to make a lot of money
What could she be doing now?
White magnolia
On the way to school
Coming home from school
Every morning and evening
I look at you passing by
As if you were Sooni herself

by Kim Young-tong

Our Prayer

Make us keep the sputtering lantern burning
and not to break a wounded reed
Make us understand
the secret of eternal life
from the pulse of blood in our veins
and realize the worth of a life
from the movement of a warm heart
Make us not discriminate
the rich and the poor
the high and the low
the learned and the ignorant
those we know well and do not know
Oh!
A human life can't be exchanged for the whole world
This supreme task of keeping the lives
of the sons and daughters of God
Let us realize how lovely it is
to feel the burdens of responsibility

by a worker of Peace Market
Written during study at night, December 1977

목   련

순이네집 담 넘어 하얀 목련꽃
한나절 햇살에도 서운하구나
돈 많이 벌겠다고 도시로 떠난
순이는 지금쯤 무얼하는지
아침저녁 학교길에 하얀 목련꽃
순이야 너를보듯 보면서간다

최 계 락   김 영 동

우리의 기원

꺼지는 등불을 꺼지지 않게 하시고
상한 갈대도 꺾지 말게 하소서
뛰노는 맥박에서 영원한 생명의
신비를 알게 하시고
따뜻한 심장의 고동에서
한 생명의 존귀를 깨닫게 하소서

돈이 많은이와 없는이를
지위가 높은이와 지위가 낮은이를
무식한이와 유식한 이를
내가 잘 아는이와 내가 잘 모르는 이를
차별하지 않게 하여 주소서

아 !
온 천하를 주고도 바꿀 수 없는 사람의 생명
하느님의 아들딸의 생명을 지키는
너무나도 이 엄청나고
벅찬 사명의 두텁고 무겁고
사랑스러움을 깨닫게 하소서.

평화시장 남자 노동자(야학하면서 씀 / 77.)

43

Night Shift

Her husband has six fingers
Four were amputated by the cutting machine
Reckon he sold each finger at 50,000 won
But he spent 200,000 won on drink
And came home empty-handed

Crying and lamenting, what's the use
She had to go to sell her labor cheap
My poor sister, what will she be doing tonight?
She must have put her name again
On the list for the night shift

To work for money is not bad
But her body is not iron
Day shift, night shift, two shifts a day
"Who wants to go on like this?" her weak voice pleads
"I am in the third stage of tuberculosis."

While she makes these clothes
Who is going to wear them
Will it be the lady of the company president
Or is it a big nose, or a Jap who will wear them
For my sister, work clothes are good enough, they say

When the puppy of the company president
Catches a cold, it is taken to the hospital
In a luxurious car
The workers' lot is to take No-Doze, Pep Pills

Anonymous

야 근

서방님의 손가락은 여섯개래요
시퍼런 절단기에 뚝뚝 짤려서
한개에 오만원씩 이십만원을
술퍼먹고 돌아오니 빈털털이래

울고 짜고 해봐야 소용있나요
막 노동판에라도 나가봐야죠
불쌍한 언니는 어떠하나요
오늘도 철야명단 올렸겠지요

돈 벌어대는 것도 좋긴하지만
무슨 통뼈 깡다구로 맨날 철야유
누군들 하고 싶어 하느냐면서
힘없이 하는 말이 폐병삼기래

이 옷을 만들며는 누가 입나요
사장님 사모님이 사서 입나요
코쟁이 쪽발이가 사서 입나요
우리들은 작업복만 어울린대요

사장님네 강아지는 감기 걸려서
포니타고 병원까지 가신다는데
우리들은 타이밍 약 사다 먹고요
시다신세 면할 날만 기다리누나

THE EXPLOITERS

What dream shall I have?
I've got nothing left.

A small elite in south Korea has become increasingly addicted to goods that require large amounts of foreign exchange. Chun Doo-hwan and all the wealthy elite have used 40,000 American soldiers and hundreds of millions of dollars of U.S. military aid to protect themselves from their own people.

A U.S. Army Base Village

Over the west mountain
tired twilight fades away
Its shadow moves as ocean waves
on worn out curtains
hung in the window
In the small room intoxicated
by darkness
what light shall I turn on?
Tonight What dream shall I have?
Under the street light
a blind man sings
unheard by anyone
The song is scattered
blinding with the noise
of cars and barking dogs
I hear the tick-tock of a watch
In no time it leaks out onto the street
Tonight What dream shall I have?
I can't hear anything
On the streets at night
strangers noisily pass by
Young women with brightly painted faces
stand restless on the sidewalks
Stars vanish one by one
to run off to the end of the sky
Tonight What dream shall I have?
I've got nothing left

Anonymous

기 지 촌

서산 마루에 시들어지는 지쳐버린 황혼이
창에 드리운 낡은 커텐위에
희미하게 넘실 거리네
어두움에 취해버린 작은 방안에
무슨 불을 밝혀둘까
오늘밤에는 무슨꿈을 꿀까 아무것도 보이지않네

가로등아래 장님의 노래 아무한테도 들리지않고
자동차 소리 개짓는 소리에
뒤섞여 흩어지네
시계소리 내귓전을 스치더니
만창 밖으로 새어나가
오늘밤에는 무슨 꿈을 꿀까 아무것도 들리지 않네

밤거리엔 낯선 사람들 떠들면서 지나가고
짙은화장의 젊은여인들이
길가에 서성대네
작은 별들이 하나둘 흩어지더니
하늘 끝으로 달아가
오늘밤에는 무슨 꿈을 꿀까 아무것도 남지않네

A Scene

Putting on the T-shirt Sooni had washed
a white soldier departed Ui-Jong-Boo
yesterday
Tonight, at the stand-up bar of Israel
by the side of the Dead Sea
he is tipping a poor daughter
of the bar-owner

Asia and Europe
Here and there
The tank battalions
may be cooking

by Shin Tong-yup

The Wind Blows

The wind blows, the wind blows
from Siberia, the wind blows
The Russian Embassy is on fire
How well it burns, how well it burns
Exhilarating, exhilarating!
Russians do nothing but
play with their watchbands
The fire blazes and water is there
but nobody tries to put it out
La la la. . . la. . .
Firemen spray gasoline instead
How well it burns, how well it burns
Exhilarating, exhilarating!
The Russians do nothing but
play with their watchbands

The wind blows, the wind blows
from the Pacific ocean, the wind blows

풍 경

순이가 빨아준 와이샤쓰를 입고
어제 의정부 떠난 백인 병사는
오늘밤, 사해(死海) 가의
이스라엘 선술집서,
주인집 가난한 처녀에게
팁을 주고,

아시아와 유우럽
이곳 저곳에서
탱크부대는 지금
밥을 짓고 있을 것이다

-신 동 엽-

바람이 분다

바람이 분다 바람이 불어
시베리아에서 불어온다
로스케 대사관에 불이 붙었다
잘 탄다 잘 탄다 신난다 신난다
로스케는 시계만 돌린다
불은 붙어도 물이 있어도
안 끈다. 라라라… 라…
소방서원은 석유 뿌린다
잘 탄다 잘 탄다
신난다 신난다

The American Embassy is on fire
How well it burns, how well it burns
Exhilarating, exhilarating!
Americans do nothing but
    chew gum
The fire blazes and water is there
but nobody tries to put it out
    La la la. . . la. . .
Firemen spray gasoline instead
How well it burns, how well it burns
Exhilarating, exhilarating!
Americans do nothing but
    chew gum

The wind blows, the wind blows
From the Japan Strait, the wind blows
The Japanese Embassy is on fire
How well it burns, how well it burns
Exhilarating, exhilarating!
Japanese do nothing but
    stamp on their geta*
The fire blazes and water is there
but nobody tries to put it out
    La la la. . . la. . .
Firemen spray gasoline instead
How well it burns, how well it burns
Exhilarating, exhilarating!
Japanese do nothing but
    stamp on their geta

The wind blows, the wind blows
from Tongbingo** the wind blows
Tongbingo village of Five Bandits*** is on fire
How well it burns, how well it burns
Exhilarating, exhilarating!
Five Bandits do nothing but
    swing their golf clubs
The fire blazes and water is there
but nobody tries to put it out
    La la la. . . la. . .

바람이 분다 바람이 불어
태평양에서 불어온다
미국 대사관에 불이 붙었다
잘 탄다 잘 탄다 신난다 신난다
미국놈은 츄잉검만 씹는다
불은 붙어도 물이 있어도
안 끈다. 라라라… 라…
소방서원은 석유 뿌린다
잘 탄다 잘 탄다
신난다 신난다

바람이 분다 바람이 불어
일본해협에서 불어 온다
일본 대사관에 불이 붙었다
잘 탄다 잘 탄다 신난다 신난다
일본놈은 게다짝만 딸락인다
불은 붙어도 물이 있어도
안 끈다. 라라라…… 라…
소방서원은 석유 뿌린다
잘 탄다 잘 탄다
신난다 신난다

바람이 분다 바람이 불어
동빙고에서 불어온다
동빙고 오적촌에 불이 붙었다
잘 탄다 잘 탄다 신난다 신난다
오적놈들 골프채만 돌린다
불은 붙어도 물이 있어도
안 끈다. 라라라…… 라…
소방서원은 석유 뿌린다
잘 탄다 잘 탄다
신난다 신난다

Firemen spray gasoline instead
How well it burns, how well it burns
Exhilarating, exhilarating!
Five Bandits do nothing but
swing their golf clubs

Anonymous

*Geta are Japanese wooden clogs.
**Tongbingo is the rich people's area in Seoul.
***The Five Bandits are from a famous Kim Chi Ha poem, representing the five power elites in Korea.

Those Who Peel the Skin

Those who peel the skin
of our people
and carve flesh from our bones
and take the skin, pound the bones
and marinate the flesh
to cook in pots to eat
Woe unto you!
In your bed you think
only of evil schemes
Villain! With powers of darkness!
You become greedy
You take away others' land
Make others' houses your own
And with the house
You make the owner your servant
And with the land
You force the owner into labor

Anonymous

이 백성의
가죽을 벗기고

이 백성의 가죽을 벗기고
뼈에서 살을 발라내는 것들
가죽을 벗기고 뼈를 바수고
고기를 저며 냄비에다 끓여 먹는 것들
망할것들 같으니라고
자리에 들어선 못된일만 궁리하고
눈만뜨면 그일을 실천에 옮기는 것들
이 악당들아, 이 권력가들아 !
탐만나면 남의 밭도 빼앗고
남의 집도 제것으로 만들며
집과 함께 집주인마저 종으로 부리고
밭과 함께 밭임자까지 부려 먹는구나

THE HOPES

Wish someone held my hand
Wish I held your hand
A high wall blocks the way between us

Bertolt Brecht once wrote to the generals that their powerful tanks had a problem: they needed drivers. Their awesome bombers had a problem: they needed mechanics. Their mighty armies had a problem: the soldiers could think.

So it is in Korea. If the multinationals, the generals, the corrupt politicians, and the wealthy industrialists could only teach the workers, the farmers, and all those who keep them in wealth not to think or dream or pray, all would be well for the exploiters.

But the workers are not machines; the farmers are not docile oxen. They spin out dreams and plans even as they produce yards of exquisite fabrics for New York, Paris and Tokyo designers.

Ah, Wish Someone Showed Me So

Ah, wish someone showed me blue sky
Ah, wish someone showed me the Milky Way
Hidden in the cloud
As if they didn't exist at all
Ah, wish someone showed me so

Ah, wish someone held my hand
Ah, wish I held your hand
A high wall blocks the way between us
Ah, wish someone held me so

Ah, wish I were green grass in the field
Ah, wish I were a pebble in the stream
Under the sky, in the field, in blowing wind
Ah, wish I became so

by Kim Min-ki

54

아하 누가 그렇게

아하 누가 푸른하늘 보여주면 좋겠네
아하 누가 은하수도 보여주면 좋겠네
구름속에 가리운듯 애당초없는듯
아하 누가 그렇게 보여주면 좋겠네

아하 누가 나의손을 잡아주면 좋겠네
아하 네가 너의 손을 잡았으면 좋겠네
높이 높이 두터운 벽가로 놓였으니
아하 누가 그렇게 잡았으면 좋겠네

아하 내가 저 들판에 풀잎이면 좋겠네
아하 내가 시냇 가에 돌멩이면 좋겠네
하늘 아래 저 들판에 부는 바람속에
아하 내가 그렇게 되었으면 좋겠네

Farewell (excerpts)

Bowing my head
I say good-bye to my poor shadow
Raising my head
I would rather look
forward to a strange place
I kiss my village, forest and
red dirt with my tears
I embrace the naked suffering

of our land for which we ought to
struggle with the whole of our selves
My home land embraces
crazy, crazy rebellions!
Strong, strong odor of dirt
fills my heart. . .

I will embrace you tightly, tightly
and say good-bye
Tall poplars run along the lonely lane
Following forest shadows that move along
the dazzling yellow dirt lane
the city slips back farther away
Good-bye, good-bye

by Kim Chi-ha

결 별

(생략)
고개를 숙여
내 초라한 그림자에 이별을 고하고
눈을 들어 이제는 차라리 낯선 곳
마을과 숲과 시뻘건 대지를 눈물로 입맞춘다
온 몸을 내던져 싸워야 할 대지의
저 벌거벗은 고통들을 끌어 안는다
미친 반역의 가슴 가득 안겨오는 고향이여
짙은, 짙은 흙냄새여, 가슴 가득히

(중략)
굳게 굳게 껴안으리라 잘있거라
키 큰 미류나무 달리는 외줄기
눈부신 황톳길 따라 움직이는 숲 그늘 따라
멀어져가는 도시여
잘 있거라 잘있거라

-김 지 하-

THE COUNTRY

It was thirty some years ago
When one day, in a glorious season
I became a refugee, not knowing why

Many, many different theories and strategies exist for the best way to reunify Korea—some say there are as many different theories as there are Koreans. But one thing is clear—all Koreans think of Korea as one country. The pain of division is great. It violates their heritage: "Everyone is the descendant of Tan-Goon!" And for many, it makes it impossible to visit relatives, and even parents, on the other side of a barrier called a boundary located on the 38th parallel. For many, this barrier was established by the superpowers for their own interests and without concern for the Korean people.

An Old Popular Song

The moon is one, the sun is one, love is one
I have one heart dedicated
to this country
How could there be two motherlands?
We are all descendants of Tan-Goon*

Water is one, the sun is one, the land is one
Mountain chains run in one
through the country
How could there be two people?
Everyone is the descendant of Tan-Goon

Anonymous

*Tan-Goon was the legendary first ruler of the Korean people.

물도 하나 해도 하나

달도 하나 해도 하나 사랑도 하나
이 나라의 바친 마음 그도 하나 이런만
하물며 조국이야 둘이 있을까 보냐
모두야 우리들은 단군의 자손

물도 하나 해도 하나 산천도 하나
이나라의 뻗친 산맥 그도 하나이런만
하물며 민족이야 둘이 있을까 보냐
모두야 이 겨레의 젊은 사나이

-흘러간 가요-

The Small Pond

There is a small pond on a high mountain
by a narrow path
with only stagnant water and no life in it
But a long time ago there lived
two pretty gold fish
One bright summer day
the two gold fish in the pond
fought against one another
and a fish floated on the water
and its flesh was rotten
and all of the pond water was rotten
and nothing lives in the pond anymore
In a small pond on a high mountain
by a narrow path
there's only stagnant water with no life

Green leaves fell one by one
floating as small boats
and sank in the deep water
Stray deer wandered in the mountain
and drank from the pond
As they raised their heads graciously
the sun set over the western mountain
and silence reigned all over the mountain
A beetle buzzed away, leaving
the pond filled with only dark water
In pained silence
many years have gone by
for the small pond on the high mountain
by a narrow path
with stagnant water and no life

by Kim Min-ki

작은 연못

깊은산 오솔길 옆 자그마한 연못엔
지금은 더러운 물만 고이고 아무것도 살지 않지만
먼 옛날 이 연못엔
예쁜 붕어 두마리
살고 있었다고 전해지지요 조그만 작은 연못
어느 맑은 여름날
연못 속에 붕어 두마리
서로 싸워 한마리는 물위에 떠오르고
그놈 살이 썩어 들어가
물도 따라 썩어 들어가
연못 속에선 아무것도 살 수 없게 되었죠
깊은 산 오솔길 옆 자그마한 연못엔
지금은 더러운 물만 고이고 아무것도 살지않죠

푸르던 나무잎이 한잎 두잎 떨어져
연못 위에 작은배 띄우다가 깊은 물에 가라 앉으면
집잃은 꽃사슴 들
산길을 헤메다가
연못을 찾아와 물을 마시고 살며시 듣게 되죠
해는 서산에 지고
저녁산은 고요한데
산 허리로 무당벌레 하나 휘의 지나간 후에
검은 물만 고인채
끝없는 세월 속을
말없이 몸짓으로 헤메다가 수많은 계절을 맞죠
깊은산 오솔길 옆 자그마한 연못엔
지금은 더러운 물만 고이고 아무것도 살지 않죠

The Wish

It is a season of splendor
When the creeks break free to run
And pussy willows bloom; the buds
New greens, break through oppressing soil
The flowers, delicate, paint scenes of joy and hope
It was the same thirty some years ago
When one day, in a glorious season
I became a refugee, not knowing why

Yes, we had thought that it was done
And that the time had come
That we could be ourselves
The hosts of our own houses, in our land
But why have I become a refugee?
What crimes have I committed
That I have had to pack up like a thief
Collecting someone else's things
In haste, perplexity, all hidden
From the neighbor's eyes
Abandoning my home, my heart
To travel like a vagabond
Loathing my luggage
In the tide of the evening darkness
We went up to Wonsan for a boat
There was no boat
At least we had a truck we'd hired in Pyong-Yang
We drove along the coast
How beautiful the beaches of the land I left!
Myong Sa-Ship-Ri, the miles of white sand
The matching miles of untainted sky and sea
The smiling infant joy of innocence, the being
With the one, the changing and unchanging
The sublime, with a being all its own
How mystically serene, the far horizon
Luring always far away
As if it were whispering "Come to me!"
And shouting "Stay!" at the same time

소　원

화창한 계절
시냇물 풀려 졸졸 달리고
버들 강아지 보송보송 싹 터 올라
파란 새싹들 대지의 압력 뚫고 고개들 무렵
어떤 날 우리는 이 화창한 계절에
까닭모를 피난민이 되어버렸다

모든 것이 끝나고
우리가 우리 땅의 주인노릇할 줄로 알았는데
피난민 노릇이란 웬 말인가?
무슨 죄를 지었기에
남의 물건 훔치듯
이웃 몰래 숨어
성급히 겨냥없이
짐보따리 싸 갖고
나의 집 나의 사랑 저바리고
저녁녘 어둠타고
뜨내기 신세가 되었는가?
지겹던 피난민 보따리여!

배를 탈까 하고 원산까지 갔으나 배가 없어
평양에서 전세낸 트럭에 다시 올라
따라 내려가는 동해안
여이고 가야하는 내 강산이여
못 잊도록 아름다운 서운함이여
명사 십 리 백사장엔
가도 가도 줄기지는 눈부신 모래
모래밭 따라
줄달음하는
하늘과 바다의 티끗 없는 푸르름
순진 무구의 어린이 웃음짓는 그 존재
변함과 불변함을
동시에 내포하는
지상(至上)의 존재, 스스로 있는 자
저 먼 수평선의 신비한 고요

We passed the pines, innumerable groves
Like parasols of green. They made my heart ache
The pains of life were born in me, so young a child
Who would normally play and laugh!

Then there was the magnitude and delicacy
Of the mountains of Keum Kang
How I wanted to jump from peak to peak
Playing hide-and-seek on each, and standing proud
I wanted to cry out to my heart's content
To listen to the trails of my own echoes
"I want to live like this!
I have the right to live like this!"
Bang, bang, bang!
It is a river in our own country
That we were forced to cross. Hoping for luck alone
We rolled our skirts and pants up to our thighs
We were desperate
Some Russian soldiers fired at us. It was
our own river. It was a time of peace
Who were they, these Russians!

Someone high up gave an order
That order made a chain
That chain bound them and us
That chain bound him and me
"Do I know him? Have we met?"
If only I had met him face-to-face
It might have been different
We could have been friends . . . who knows?
We had no chance to try
Even before we could question them
They shot. We were their targets
Russians firing on Koreans
It is absurd
Is it a game? But how dangerous, and real
And yet I didn't envy them their posts
Those soldiers dangling at the end of the chain
And yet, at my endlessly vulnerable position
I wept

항상 저 멀리 나를 부르며
"내게로 오라"고 속삭이듯
동시에 "그곳에 머물어라" 고함치듯

푸른 양산 펴 놓은듯 올망졸망
수 없이 지나가는 솔나무 숲
내 가슴에 일어나는 통증있어
인생고의 쓴잔 맛보는
어린 나이여
응당 놀고 웃어야할 어린 나이여

웅장 교묘의 금강산 봉우리
봉우리마다 뛰어 건너며
숨바꼭질이라도 해 봤으면
봉우리 정상에 우뚝 서서
"나는 이렇게 살고 싶다
나도 이렇게 살 권리가 있다."
싫것 고함치며
산울림 소리라도 들어봤으면

팡, 팡, 팡....
우리나라 강물인데
건너야만 하는 이 강요
요행만 바라는 이 강요
치마와 바지를 허벅지까지 올려 부치고
처절하게 가는 강요의 행진
우리나라 우리 강 우리가 건느는데
전시도 아닌 평화 시절인데
노서아 군인들이 총질한다

노서아군이란 무엇인가?
히로시마 나가사끼 며칠 후에
일본의 패배가 명확해진 후
그 바로 며칠 후에 일본에게
선전포고하고
자본주의 자들의 치열한 전쟁속에
다른 한 자본주의 세력에 동조하여 말려 들었다
우리를 해방시킨 위대한 군대라고 자칭하며
무장도 않고 의지할데 없는
양민들에게 총질하였다
자유롭게 살고파
우리 강물 건느는게 죄목이란다

On the other side at last, we reached a hill
Escaping narrowly
We fled, were refugees, not knowing why
Just sitting on a southern hill
Just like a northern hill
I could not laugh at the triumph of escape
But only weep again
My laughter having been repressed
Before I was born

Help! Oh, help me and my people!
Someone said that all the refugees
Should go to the camp—a sea of people
I asked, "Is all of north Korea down here now?"
I saw Yankee soldiers for the first time in my life
They all had shiny shoes
Clean, pressed uniforms
They were clean themselves
Just out of the bath, perhaps
They all chewed gum relentlessly
They all held strange machines
They were spraying us with powder, DDT, as if to say
"We'll rid you of the bugs and germs
You are carrying from the north."
As if to say, as well, "This rite
Will authorize you to live in the south
Like us civilized and free."
Was this their way of humanitarian benevolence?
We were made all white, baptized from head to toe
All white as flour-packers or as homeless nomads
Roaming in the dust. Weren't we the same
Once called the bourgeoisie
Who have been pushed into this plight?
Some bourgeoisie! We whose very lives depend
On excess grain from the USA!
Do I thank them? Curse them?
Oh, I cannot distinguish friend from foe!

This is how my "Freedom" and my "Dignity" began
This is how my "Politics" awoke in me
As my knowledge grows, our plight seems more difficult
As the dictators sing of "democracy"

높은 곳에서 명령이 내려
그 명령은 고랑처럼 줄줄이 이어
그와 나를 함께 묶어 버렸네
"나는 그를 아는가?
우리는 서로 만난 일이라도 있었는가?"
그와 내가 얼굴과 얼굴 대하여
만난 일이 있었더라면
형편이 달라졌을지 모를 노릇
원수가 아니고 친구이었을지 모를 노릇

그럴 기회는 주어지잖고
왜 그렇냐고 물어볼 겨를도 없이
그들은 우리에게 발포하였고
우리는 그들의 조격대상이 되어 버렸다
한국인에게 총질하는 노서아인들
이야말로 터무니 없는 일이 아닌가
이것은 장난인가
장난치고는 너무나 위험한 현실

하지만 나는 그네들 선 자리가 부럽지 않다
명령의 쇠고랑 끄트마리에
댕그렁거리는 그들 신세
하지만 내 형편도 낳을게 없다
끝없이 허약한 우리 형편
끝없이 울어야할 우리 형편

마침내 도달한 피안의 언덕
까딱하면 놓질번한 그 언덕
우리는 도망자요, 피난민이요,
무슨 연고로 이 신세가 되었을까
북쪽과 다름없는
남쪽 언덕에 주저앉아
도주의 성공을 웃기보다는
울어야했던 나의 신세
내가 태어나기 전서부터
내 웃음은 억눌림을 당해 있었다

도우소서! 나와 내 민족 도우소서
"피난민은 다 한 곳에 몰여라"
바다처럼 몰인 사람
마치 북쪽 모든 백성 다 밀려온 듯

They call "communist" whoever speaks of
"Rights," "justice," and "freedom"
And innocents are found, imprisoned, tortured, killed
The schemes are devilish!
To reinforce their power
They loan us money, making their pockets fat
With snow-balling interest
While the weight of our country's debt
Strangles the poor
How dangerous this "anti-communism" is
How mutable!

"Free the poor! Free the oppressed!
Free them from the grips of a thousand demons!
Jesus set the example: we are merely following
His steps." They say: "You are the reds.
You're communists, and dangerous."
The Christians exiled by the Kim regime
Are harrassed by the Park/Chun regime
Where can we turn now
With the Red Sea and the desert before us?
Oh, God help our people to build a bridge
Over the Red Sea and straighten the road in the desert
To come out victorious from the hell
Of hatred and division, to be led in the land
Of love, unity and peace!

Spring has returned again
Thirty-five springs since I crossed that wretched border
The thirty-eighth parallel
So arbitrary a division in our history
O Korea, where we each are born
With marks of death, indelible
Yes, it is another spring, another hope
My days are turning round and round, and I can see
The original point, but cannot get to it somehow
My enemies are too many and too strong
Oh, Korea! I suffer in my love for you!
Let the day come, let me see it
All—before my eyes, which have shed so many tears
Have finally closed

by Lee Sun-ai

평생에 처음보는 양키 군인들
모두들 반짝이는 군화 신었고
반듯하게 줄진 군복입고
금새 욕탕에서 나온듯 깨끗하고
모두들 추잉검 짝짝 씹으며
이상한 기계들 손에 들고
쾌재라 뿌리는 DDT공세
"북쪽에서 가져오는
이와 병균 모두 제거해 주마"
그들은 또 이렇게 말하는듯 하였다
"이것은 우리처럼 문명하고 자유롭게
남쪽에서 살기를 허락하는 의식이라."
이것이 그들의 인도주의 자선인가
머리부터 발끝까지 핧애진 우리들

밀가루 봉지 싸는 작업부들인양
하얀 몬지속에 방황하는 유랑민인양
모두들 받은 흰가루 세례
북쪽에선 우리를 부르죠아지라고 하지 않았나?
미국 잉여 농산물에 의지하여
연명해 가야하는 기형 부르죠아지
나는 미국에게 감사해야 하는가
저주해야 하는가
친구인지 적인지도 분간하기 어렵구나

이렇게 내 "자유"와 "존엄"은 시작됐다
이렇게 "정치"는 내 속에 눈떴다
세상을 알수록 우리 신세는 더 어렵게 보인다
독재자들이 "민주주의"를 노래한다
"인권, 정의, 자유"를 말하면 빨갱이라 한다
죄 없는 자들이 투옥 당하고
고문 처형 욕을 본다
사악한 짓
부강한 나라들은 그들 세력을 굳히려고
우리에게 빚주고 이자로 살찐다
점점 뿔어가는 높은 이자율
이 나라 빚 중량에
가난한 백성들은 목이 졸린다
위험한 "반공주의!"
실속없는 "민주주의"

"가난한 자를 놓아 주어라!"
"억압 받은 자를 놓아 주어라!"
"천만 악귀의 손아귀에서 풀어 주어라!"
"예수가 본 세웠다
우리는 그의 뒤를 · 따를 나름이다."
"너희는 위험한 공산주의자들이다."
김일성에게 쫓겨난 예수쟁이들
박 · 전 정권에게 핍박받는다
우리는 어디서 도움을 받나?
홍해와 사막이 우리 앞에 깔렸으니
주여 도우소서
우리 민족으로 다리를 지어
홍해에 걸고
사막길 바르게 하옵소서
증오와 분단의 이 지옥서 빠져나와
사랑과 통일 평화의 나라로
승리로 이르도록하여 주소서

또 한 봄은 오고
저주의 삼팔선
넘은지도 삼십오년
저주의 삼팔선
터무니없는 분단의 역사
지울 수 없는 주검의 표적갖고
우리 각자 생을 얻은 한국이여!
지금은 또하나의 봄철
또 하나의 희망
내 날은 뱅뱅 겉돌기만 하고
환히 보이는 원점엔
도달할 길 막막해
우리 적들은 너무 많고 너무 강하다
오, 한국이여!
나는 너를 사랑하여 고통하노라
그날이여 오소서
허다한 눈물 흘린 나의 눈이
마침내 감겨지기 그 이전에
그 날을 보게 하소서

WHAT YOU CAN DO

Many ways are open to share these poems with others and to share in·a small, personal way the lives of the poets and all Korean people. Our suggestions vary from making sure your library carries this book to community programs. Here are some ideas that may be helpful to you:

1. Have a special Korean night in your community. Such an evening might include:

    a. a Korean dinner (the Committee for a New Korea Policy can provide recipes for groups for $1 including postage—see address below)

    b. a poetry reading using community talent

    c. a speaker (see list of organizations below which can help provide speakers)

    d. special Korean games for the child care room may be found in *In Celebration of Korea* and *Children's Games from Many Lands* published by Friendship Press Inc., New York, N.Y.

2. Use this poetry in your church service and Sunday School classes. The Southeast Asia Resource Center (address below) can provide a special liturgy for your use ($1 including postage). Make sure that your church devotes at least one Sunday during the year to the situation in Korea.

3. Reprint one of the poems in this book in your newsletter or on the back cover of your church bulletin.
you must credit Friendship Press Inc., New York, N.Y.!)

4. Support the families of political prisoners through your prayers and with a donation. The Office for East Asia and the Pacific of the National Council of Churches of Christ (NCCCUSA) provides assistance to the National Council of Churches in Korea which gives legal assistance to political prisoners and help to their families. Checks can be made out to "NCCCUSA" and sent to the Office of East Asia and the Pacific, Room 616, 475 Riverside Drive, New York, NY 10115 and designated "Support for Korean Prisoner Families."

5. There are many organizations which work on Korea. Some of them have regular publications: most can help with providing speakers, expert information, and updates on the current situation in Korea. In some cases, a specific name is mentioned to get quicker attention.

ORGANIZATIONS

North American Coalition on Human Rights in Korea, 110 Maryland Ave. NE, Washington, DC 20002. Telephone: (202) 546-4304. N.Y. office: 475 Riverside Drive, #1538, New York, NY 10115. Telephone: (212) 870-3693. Coalition of national and regional religious organizations; coordinates action groups; represents these concerns in Washington, D.C.; publishes newsletter; furnishes clipping service; and provides taped weekly telephone updates. (202) 546-NEWS.

Council for Democracy in Korea, P.O. Box 3657, Arlington, Va., 22203. Telephone: (202) 265-9808. Sponsors seminars and publishes newsletter.

United Movement for Democracy in Korea, 1809 Monroe St. NW, Washington, DC 20010. Organization of Korean residents in the United States and Canada to support the democratic movement in Korea.

Committee for a New Korea Policy, 221 Central Ave., Albany, NY 12206. Telephone: (518) 434-4037. Citizen action group. Publishes periodic pamphlets.

Southeast Asia Resource Center (Don Luce), 198 Broadway, New York, NY 10038. Telephone: (212) 964-6730. Provides speakers and resource materials on East and Southeast Asia.

East Asia and the Pacific Desk, National Council of Churches of Christ, 475 Riverside Drive, New York, NY 10115. Telephone: (212) 870-2371. Coordinates the official relationships of the Protestant church with Korea. In addition, each denomination has a person assigned to work on Korean concerns.

Church Committee on Human Rights in Asia, 1821 W. Cullerton, Chicago, IL 60608. Telephone: (312) 226-0675. Citizen action group. Publishes "Asian Rights Advocate."

American Friends Service Committee (Roberta Levenbach), 1501 Cherry St., Philadelphia, PA 19102. Telephone: (215) 241-7000. Seminars and working on book on Korea. Special interest in question of reconciliation between north and south.

Korea Support Committee, P.O. Box 11425, Oakland, CA 94611. Telephone (415) 753-5432. Action group in Bay area oriented toward labor and military issues.

Washington State Korean Human Rights Council, 1713 214th St. SW, Lynwood, WA 98036. Telephone: (206) 776-6888. Regional coordinating body for churches and other action groups in the Northwest.

Canada-Asia Working Group, 11 Madison Ave., Toronto, Ontario, Canada M5R 252, (416) 924-9351. Church-sponsored action group with regular seminars and publications on Canadian relations with Korea, Taiwan and the Philippines.